WORLD OF DINOSAURS

WITH 4D AUGMENTED REALITY EXPERIENCE

3D ANIMATED DINOSAURS ON YOUR MOBILE DEVICE

for more info and free app please visit:
www.redfrogwebsolutions.co.uk/World-of-Dinosaurs

Leszek Tomczakowski

Red Frog Web Solutions LTD

Author: Leszek Tomczakowski

Content design: Leszek Tomczakowski, Patryk Tomczakowski

Picture research: Leszek Tomczakowski, Anna Tomczakowska, Patryk Tomczakowski

Proof Reader: Glen Pearson

Copyright © 2017 Red Frog Web Solutions LTD

Free apps on:

www.redfrogwebsolutions.co.uk/World-of-Dinosaurs

WORLD OF DINOSAURS
with 4D augmented reality experience

10 animated dinosaurs: Megalodon, Plesiosaurus, Stegosaurus, Tyranosaurus, Triceratops, Carnotaurus, Pteranodon, Velociraptor, *Quetzalcoatlus*.

MEGALODON

The perfect predator. It reigned in the waters of our planet from 15 to 1.5 million years ago. It hunted for large prey animals, mostly sharks and whales. The Megalodon would have looked very similar to a modern Great White Shark.

The reproduction of Megalodons was different to modern sharks. Megalodons gave birth to live young which were up to 2 meters long.

The area of distribution of these prehistoric sharks was very vast. Megalodons lived in the waters of the Americas, Europe, Africa, Australia and Asia.

The Megalodon's jaws were roughly 2 meters in diameter. Megalodons had 4 different types of teeth in its jaw spanning across 4 rows. A total of 276 teeth.. The biting force of the jaws could reach up to 18 tonnes, enough to break open the skull of a whale. In comparison, the biting force of a Great White Shark is 1.8 tonnes.

Megalodons were the kings of the oceans. Their ability to adapt to environmental conditions was almost perfect. This is shown by the fact that modern sharks have not changed much over millions of years, similar to crocodiles. Why did they become extinct? There are many theories. The most probable one is climate change: cooling the oceans as well as causing gradual extinction of tropical whales which were Megalodon's main food source. But maybe none of the theories are true and Megalodons are still alive in deep oceans. There are many legends about giant sharks being seen by sailors.

The size of the Megalodons is quite difficult to establish because a backbone has never been found. The only part that has been preserved until now is their teeth, which are very similar to Great White Sharks' teeth but much bigger. Based on these teeth, scientists estimate the shark could reach a length of 17 meters (56 ft) and weigh up to 60 tonnes. This would make it one of the largest predators that have ever lived on earth.

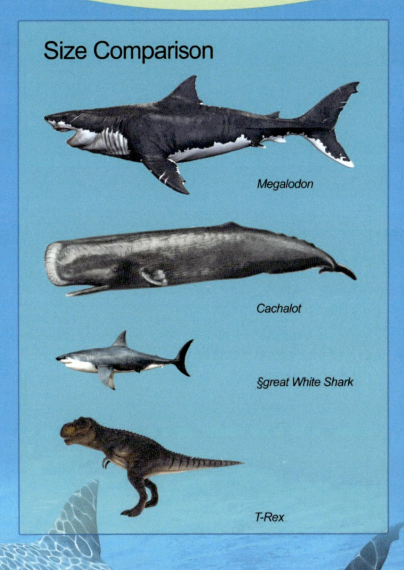

Size Comparison

Megalodon

Cachalot

§great White Shark

T-Rex

Mosasaurus

Mosasaurus ('lizard of the Meuse River') was an aquatic lizard that lived in the waters of North America, Eastern Europe and New Zealand about 70-66 million years ago. It reached up to 17 meters in length and 17 tonnes in weight. As with most mosasaurids, its limbs ended in flippers, the front ones being larger than the rear. It lived just under the surface of the ocean, hunting for turtles, smaller mosasaurs, fish and pterosaurs.

Mosasaurus most likely attacked its prey suddenly with great speed, eating it in a very short time. It could swallow a shark several meters long, whole. Its jaws were equipped with massive, sharp, pointed teeth that it could also use to hold its prey. Its eyes were fixed on the sides of its head, so it could not see three dimensionally. This meant that Mosasaurus could not judge the distance to its prey by sight. Instead, it had very good hearing, a split tongue that could recognise scents and nerves running down the sides of its body that could sense the pressure changes caused by passing animals.

Mosasaurus were territorial animals, defending their personal areas from other species. Even in the mating period, after a brief encounter the male would still drive females out of its own territory.

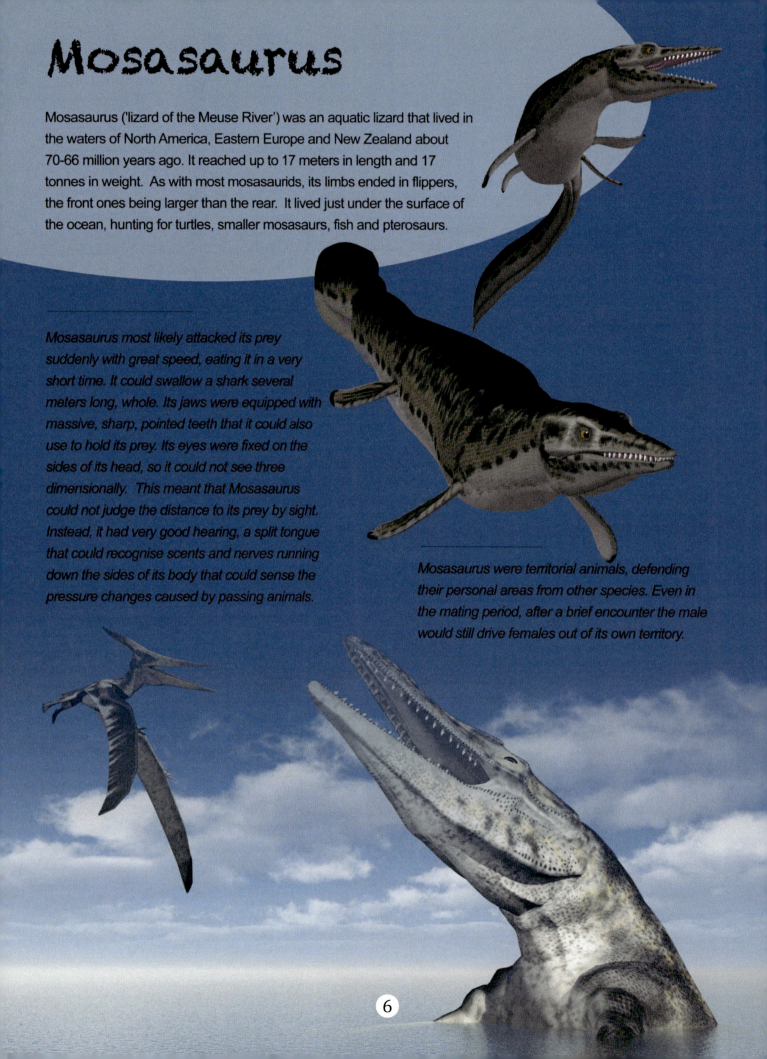

PLESIOSAURUS

Plesiosaurs dominated the waters of our planet 220-60 million years ago. They were found in water basins and were between 2-15 meters in length (6-50 feet).

Plesiosaurs were carnivores. They had extremely sharp teeth with strong jaws and hunted mainly fish and cephalopods.

Although scientists unequivocally claimed that Plesiosaurs went extinct millions of years ago, there have been many legends about these reptiles.
People have claimed to see lake and sea monsters all over the world fitting their description.

The most popular legend is the Loch Ness Monster or 'Nessie'. Humans have explored less than 5% of the world's oceans, so there is still a lot to discover. One example is the fish Letimeria, thought to be extinct for 60 million years. However, a live specimen was caught off the coast of South Africa in 1938.

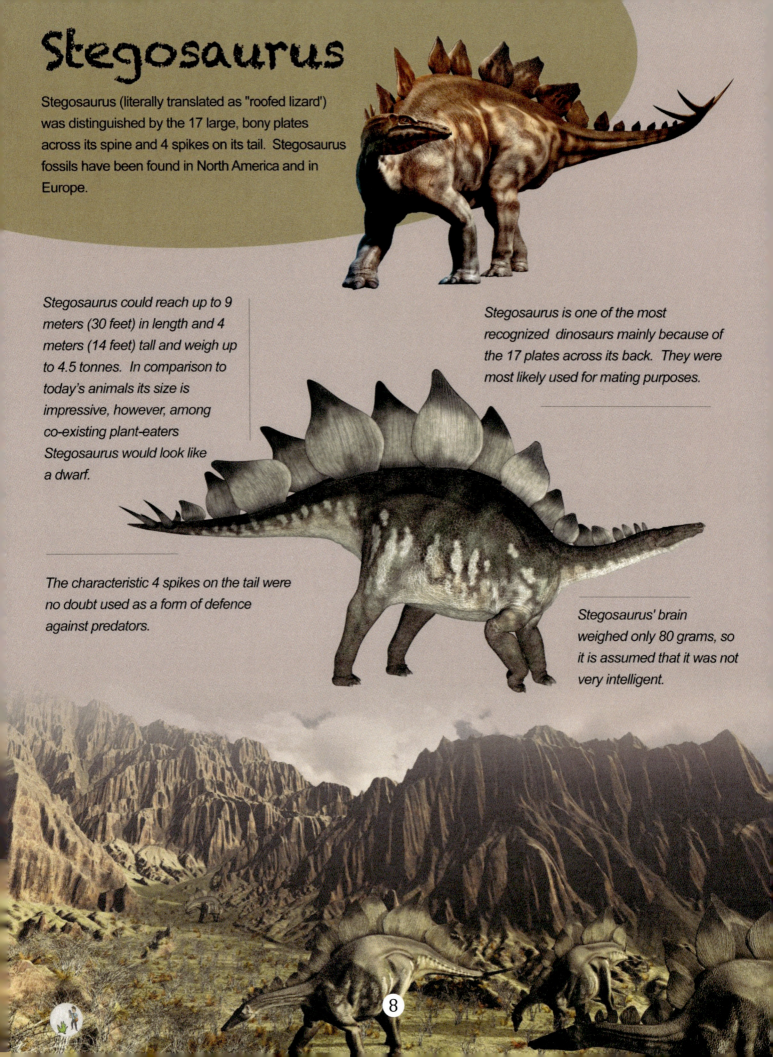

Stegosaurus

Stegosaurus (literally translated as "roofed lizard') was distinguished by the 17 large, bony plates across its spine and 4 spikes on its tail. Stegosaurus fossils have been found in North America and in Europe.

Stegosaurus could reach up to 9 meters (30 feet) in length and 4 meters (14 feet) tall and weigh up to 4.5 tonnes. In comparison to today's animals its size is impressive, however, among co-existing plant-eaters Stegosaurus would look like a dwarf.

Stegosaurus is one of the most recognized dinosaurs mainly because of the 17 plates across its back. They were most likely used for mating purposes.

The characteristic 4 spikes on the tail were no doubt used as a form of defence against predators.

Stegosaurus' brain weighed only 80 grams, so it is assumed that it was not very intelligent.

Kentrosaurus

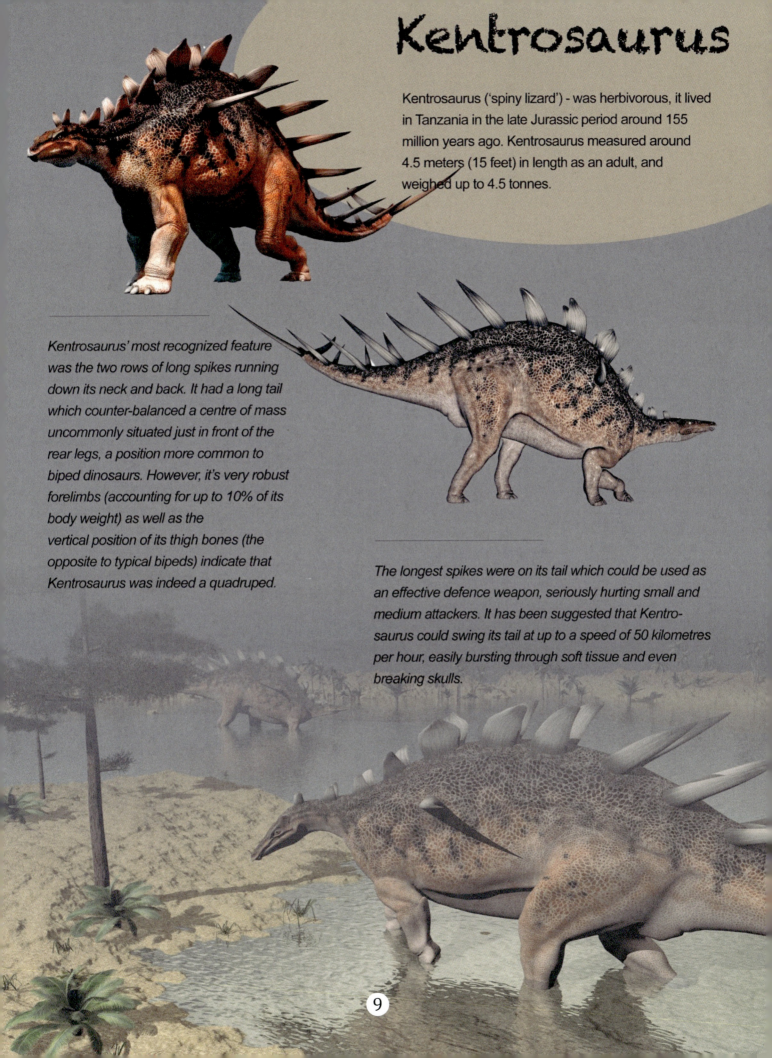

Kentrosaurus ('spiny lizard') - was herbivorous, it lived in Tanzania in the late Jurassic period around 155 million years ago. Kentrosaurus measured around 4.5 meters (15 feet) in length as an adult, and weighed up to 4.5 tonnes.

Kentrosaurus' most recognized feature was the two rows of long spikes running down its neck and back. It had a long tail which counter-balanced a centre of mass uncommonly situated just in front of the rear legs, a position more common to biped dinosaurs. However, it's very robust forelimbs (accounting for up to 10% of its body weight) as well as the vertical position of its thigh bones (the opposite to typical bipeds) indicate that Kentrosaurus was indeed a quadruped.

The longest spikes were on its tail which could be used as an effective defence weapon, seriously hurting small and medium attackers. It has been suggested that Kentrosaurus could swing its tail at up to a speed of 50 kilometres per hour, easily bursting through soft tissue and even breaking skulls.

T-Rex

Tyrannosaurus Rex (T-Rex) – was one of the biggest land predators of all time. It lived between 66 and 60 million years ago. The biggest could reach 12.5 meters (40 feet) in length and weigh almost 7 tonnes. Tyrannosaurus lived in the Americas, India and China.

Tyrannosaurs had a very well-developed sense of smell and eyesight. They could spot their prey from several kilometers away. Their sense of smell was 100 times better than today's sniffer dogs. Their olfactory lobes were the most developed among other animals living in that era.

Tyrannosaurs had powerful jaws. Their biting force could reach up to 6 tonnes. This made them one of the most superior land animals to ever live on earth. In comparison, the biting force of the human jaw is about 70 kg.

Front limbs of the Tyrannosaurus Rex were small, with 2 clawed fingers at its ends. The use of these still puzzles scientists to this day. They probably helped in keeping balance.

The Tyrannosaur's tail was a counterbalance to its powerful head and also helped it to move quickly. Computer simulations suggest that Tyrannosaurs could have moved at 40 kilometers per hour (24.85 miles per hour).

Tarbosaurus

T-Rex was not the only representative of tyrannosaurid. In Asian forests the Tarbosaurus reigned. It lived in the area now known as Mongolia, China and Korea around 70-65 million years ago. It looked very much like its relative from North America.

Tarbosaurus was slightly smaller than T-Rex. The biggest fossils that have been found were 12 meters long (compared to 12.3 meters - T-Rex) and weighed around 6 tonnes. It was at the top of the food chain in its environment.

The large head of Tarbosaurus contained strong jaws housing 60 extremely large and powerful teeth with a biting force of up to 7 tonnes. It had the smallest front limbs among all the tyrannosaurids, so small that they could not reach its muzzle.

It looked similar to T-Rex and its sense of smell was equally good. But there were also many differences. One being its stiffer jaw which was probably better suited to killing large prey.

Triceratops

Triceratops was a prehistoric rhinoceros with a parrot-like beak. It was a massive herbivore of 8-9 meters in length and weighed 6-12 tonnes. It lived 68 to 65 million years ago in today's North America.

The triceratops had one of the biggest heads amongst all of the dinosaurs.

They mainly ate plants that grew low on the ground using their strong, toothless beak but they could also reach the higher green parts of trees by bending them with their horns.

Triceratopses probably lived in herds, like today's buffalo. Although individual fossils are usually found there have also been several groups of fossils discovered together.

Their horns were used to defend against predators, as well as during mating fights and to bend larger plants.

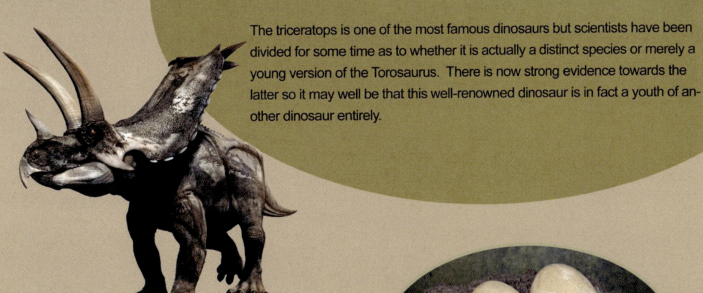

The triceratops is one of the most famous dinosaurs but scientists have been divided for some time as to whether it is actually a distinct species or merely a young version of the Torosaurus. There is now strong evidence towards the latter so it may well be that this well-renowned dinosaur is in fact a youth of another dinosaur entirely.

The Triceratops was a quadruped, its 4 legs resembling those of an elephant.

Triceratopses, like most dinosaurs, were egg-bearing. The female would build a nest where it would lay them.

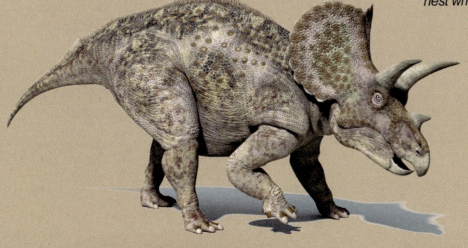

The triceratops, had a strong, toothless beak, used to pick up low growing plants.

Carnotaurus

Carnotaurus ('meat-eating bull') lived in the area of today's North America 72-69.9 million years ago. It was a bipedal predator which measured 7-8 meters (23- 26 feet) in length and weighed around 1.35 tonnes. Its distinguishing feature was its thick horns that were not seen on any other carnivores.

Scientists are unsure of the function of Carnotaurus' horns. Its muscular neck and rigid spine suggest that it could have used them like the modern ram in mating fights. It is also possible that the horns helped in killing its prey, if so, it would have been the exception in the animal world.

It is not exactly clear what these dinosaurs ate. Some studies indicate that they were able to hunt large animals, but they probably ate small vertebrates. Their jaws were capable of quick but not strong bites, similar to modern crocodiles that hunt for small prey.

Carnotaurus' arms were proportionally shorter and robust, the forearm was only a quarter of the size of the upper arm. Its legs, on the other hand, were long and slender. Their bone structure and muscularity suggest that it was a very fast animal. It is possible that this dinosaur was one of the fastest large predators.

Albertaceratops

Albertaceratops ('Alberta horned face') had large curved horns at the end of its skull and long horns at its brow, unusual for ceratopses. It is estimated that it was up to 5.8 meters (19 feet) in length and 3.5 tonnes in weight.

However, like other ceratopses it was an herbivore, with a large, bony frill and parrot-like beak. It had a round body and was quadrupedal.

Albertaceratops lived in the late Cretaceous Period. It was named after Alberta, the region in Canada where its fossils were found.

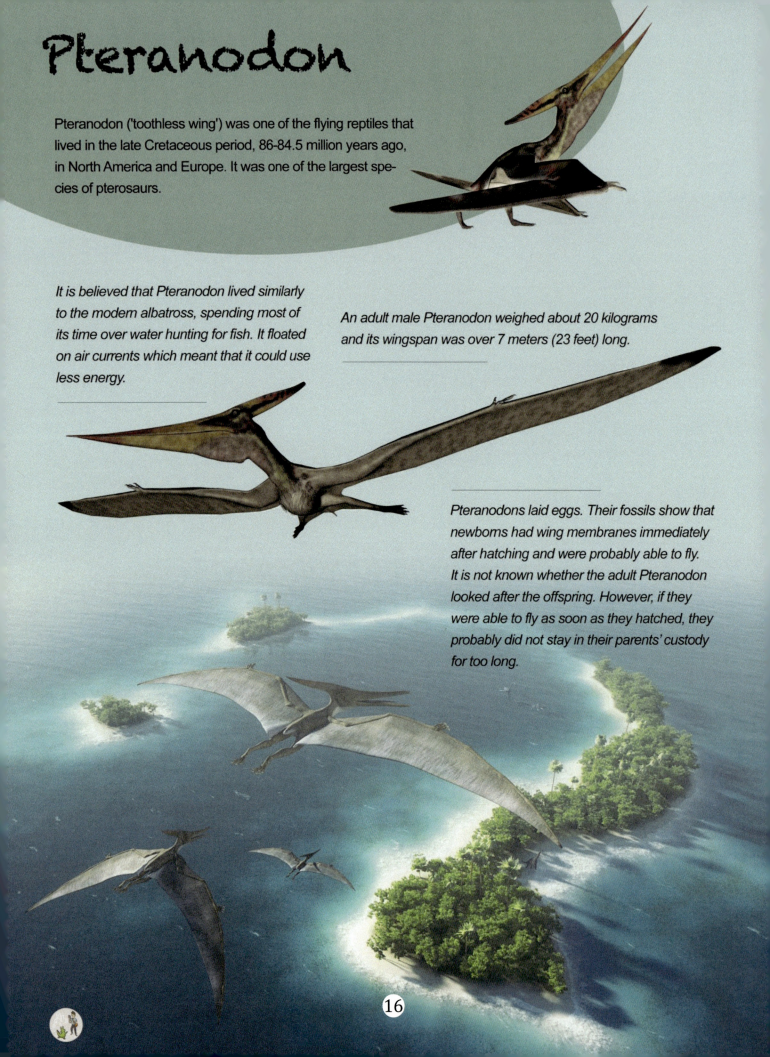

Pteranodon

Pteranodon ('toothless wing') was one of the flying reptiles that lived in the late Cretaceous period, 86-84.5 million years ago, in North America and Europe. It was one of the largest species of pterosaurs.

It is believed that Pteranodon lived similarly to the modern albatross, spending most of its time over water hunting for fish. It floated on air currents which meant that it could use less energy.

An adult male Pteranodon weighed about 20 kilograms and its wingspan was over 7 meters (23 feet) long.

Pteranodons laid eggs. Their fossils show that newborns had wing membranes immediately after hatching and were probably able to fly. It is not known whether the adult Pteranodon looked after the offspring. However, if they were able to fly as soon as they hatched, they probably did not stay in their parents' custody for too long.

Amargasaurus

Amargasaurus ('La Amarga lizard') was a sauropod. It lived in the Early Cretaceous period (129.4-122.46 million years ago) in the area of today's Argentina. It was relatively small for a sauropod, reaching up to 10 meters (33 feet) in length and weighing 2.6 tonnes.

Amargasaurus was an herbivore. It was quadrupedal, most likely unable to stand on its hind legs alone, with a body-build indicative of a slow-moving animal.

It had distinguishing tall spines running in two rows down its neck and back. However, when it comes to their function scientists have many hypotheses as to their role. One is that they served to set the hierarchy in the herd, another that they deterred or intimidated other predators. They could also be used as a weapon, skewering enemies on the spikes in the manner of the modern giant sable antelope or Arabian oryx. Finally, some scientists claim that they contained an air sac, connected to the lungs as part of the respiratory system.

According to Bakker, (a researcher in 1986) the construction of Armagasaurus' nostrils, together with the thick surrounding bones and close formation of a well-built occipital region suggest that Amagasaurus may have had a trunk.

Velociraptor

Velociraptor ('swift seizer') was a bipedal theropod from the family of dromaeosaurids. It lived 75-71 million years ago in the area of today's Mongolia. Most likely it was warm-blooded as indicated by its similarity to modern birds. It had large feet with three strongly curved claws, the longest reaching up to 6 centimetres, used to kill its prey.

Velociraptor in real life was much smaller than the one that is known to the public from Jurassic Park. It was 2 meters (7 feet) in length, 0.5 meters (1.6 feet) tall at the hips and it only weighed up to 15 kilograms.

Some Velociraptor bones have been found containing 'quill knobs' (notches where feathers are anchored to bone) indicating that Velociraptor was covered with feathers and it may have led an arboreal life.

Gigantspinosaurus

Gigantspinosaurus ('Giant-spined lizard') comes from the Stegosaur family of dinosaurs. It lived in the late Jurassic period around 152-145 million years ago in the area of today's China.

Similar to Stegosaurus and Kentrosaurus with its two rows of spikes on its back, Gigantspinosaurus' distinguishing feature was two larger, pointed spikes growing on both sides of its body.

Its fossils were found in China in the Sichuan Province amongst the Shaximiao rock formations, an area known for many fossil discoveries.

Gigantspinosaurus was around 4 metres (14 feet) long, 1.7 metres (5.5 feet) tall and weighed around 700 kilograms. Gigantspinosaurus was an herbivore.

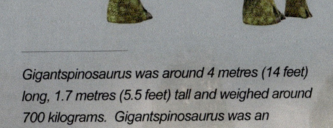

Quetzalcoatlus

Quetzalcoatlus ('feathered serpent god') was a large pterosaur that lived in the Late Cretaceous period in today's North America.

At first it was mistakenly suggested that Quetzalcoatlus ate fish like today's gulls. However, its neck wasn't flexible enough and it was found that it was very well adapted to walk on land, its fossils being found 400 kilometres from the nearest coastline. It is now believed that it hunted for small vertebrae, similar to today's storks.

Quetzalcoatlus was one of the largest flying animals ever known, being the height of a giraffe. Its wingspan was 10-12 meters (33-36 feet) and their surface area was around 5m2. Due to the size of its wings, flying mainly consisted of utilising vertical air currents. Some researchers suggest that Quetzalcoatlus was a great aviator, capable of flying for 13,000 kilometres at a time. Potentially flying at speeds of 130 kilometres per hour it could reach altitudes of up to 4,600 meters (15,000 feet). Other researchers think that these estimates are too high but even their lower estimates still tastify to the excellent adaptation of this pterosaur to flight.

Brachiosaurus

Brachiosaurus ('arm lizard') has a name derived from the fact that its front limbs are much longer than the hind ones. Brachiosaurus was an herbivore sauropod living in the late Jurassic period in regions of today's North America. It measured around 22-27 meters (72- 88 feet) in length, weighed 28-40 tons and it was 13 meters (42 feet) tall, (or 6 meters / 19 feet to its shoulders).

Brachiosaurus most likely ate foliage from high up on conifers and tree ferns, maybe about 120kg a day. It had an extremely long neck, its head could reach over 9 meters (30 feet) above the ground. It could not chew its food due to its disproportionately small head so during eating Brachiosaurus' jaw made simple vertical movements and its teeth were arranged in a way most likely used to crop and nip the vegetation. It is possible that its digestion was supported by swallowing stones similar to modern birds and crocodiles.

In the past, scientists suggested that such gigantic animals could only live by being partially submerged in water. However, today it is thought that Brachiosaurus was indeed able to live on land unsupported.

Ankylosaurus

Ankylosaurus was an armoured dinosaur that lived at the end of the Cretaceous Period, 68-65.5 million years ago, in North America. It measured 6.25 meters (20.5 feet) long, 1.5 meters (5.3 feet) wide and 1.7 meters (5.6 feet) tall and weighed 6 tonnes. It was quadrupedal, although its hind limbs were longer than the front ones.

Ankylosaurus was an herbivore. Its teeth were small in comparison to the size of its whole body. It had a skull low and triangular in shape with 4 horns in the shape of pyramids.

The body of Ankylosaurus was covered in armour plates and bony half-rings. On the end of its tail was a large club which it used in defence. When it waved this club tail the force generated was capable of breaking bones.

Sauropelta

Sauropelta ('lizard shield') was a nodosaurid dinosaur that lived in the area of today's North America from 115 to 110 million years ago (the Early Cretaceous Period). It had a similar weight to the modern black rhinoceros, although it was actually smaller. This was due to extensive, bony armour and long spikes on its neck.

An herbivore, Sauropelta was about 5 meters (17.1 feet) in length and weighed 1.5 tonnes. Its distinguishing feature was a long tail which constituted half the length of its body, containing probably 50 vertebrae. It had two rows of spines running down its neck, with very large ones in the vicinity of the shoulder blade.

Apatosaurus

Apatosaurus ('deceptive lizard'), lived in today's North America during the late Jurassic period. It was one of the biggest land animals to have ever lived on Earth.
It reached up to 20 metres (68-75 feet) in length and 23 tonnes in weight.

To this day scientists are not sure how Apatosaurus as well as other animals of its size could breathe. It could not have a normal reptile's respiratory system because it would not be able to provide enough air to its lungs. It is suggested that its respiratory system was similar to that found in birds that use additional air sacs but it is more likely that there is no known equivalent in today's animal world for comparison.

To this day it is unknown how Apatosaurus was able to provide adequate amount of food to feed such a giant body. It is most likely that it was grazing constantly with very few rest breaks.

Diabloceratops

Diabloceratops lived in the late Cretaceous Period in the area of today's North America. It was a medium sized ceratopsian that could reach up to 5.5 meters (18 feet) in length. Its name refers to the horns on its neck shield, derived from the Spanish word Diablo meaning 'devil' and the Latinised Greek word Ceratops (the usual word used to name all other ceratopsians) meaning 'horned face'.

Diabloceratops was one of the earliest living ceratopsians and was an herbivore. It had a typical parrot-like beak which it used to crop low-growing vegetation. Similar to other ceratopsians, it had a large neck frill made of bone featuring characteristic horns on top. It was quadrupedal, its limbs resembling those of an elephant.

Spinosaurus

Spinosaurus ('spine lizard') lived 106 – 93.5 million years ago in today's North Africa. It was up to 18 meters (59 feet) in length and 6 meters (19 feet) tall and it weighed up to 7-9 tonnes. Its distinctive features were a sail-like structure of spines along its back and a long muzzle.

Spinosaurus gained its popularity thanks to the third part of Jurassic Park, where it defeats T-Rex himself.

It is not clear what the Spinosaurus ate. Long jaws, high nostrils and conical teeth suggests that it was mainly fish. This is also confirmed by fish scales found in the stomach of its relative Baryonyx. It is also possible that Spinosaurus ate small animals including carrion. A few scientists suggest that it preyed on large animals using its large front limbs that ended in strong claws.

Spinosaurus had distinctive high spines which grew up to 1.65 meters (5.4 feet) long, which were long extensions of the vertebrae and were most likely connected by skin which formed a sail-like structure. It is also possible that they were connected by muscle. There are no doubts as to its function, thought to be the cooling of its body as well as scaring off attackers.

Dilophosaurus

Dilophosaurus was a dinosaur that lived 200 -191 million years ago (at the beginning of the Jurassic Period) in the area of today's USA (Arizona), Poland and Sweden. It was 7 meters (23 feet) long and weighed 400 kilograms. Its distinguishing feature was 2 half-crest combs at the top of its skull.

Dilophosaurus was an agile predator with strong hind limbs and small front limbs.
Scientists are divided about how it caught food due to the weak connection between the jaw and the skull. Some say that its skull was equipped with a system of jaw muscles acting as levers that helped it hunt, similar to other reptiles. Others claim that the loose jaw joint would have made it impossible to catch and subdue prey, Dilopho-saurus resorting to scavenging carrion instead.

Dilophosaurus gained fame by appearing in Jurassic Park, although it was represented poorly. It was shown as a small, venomous dinosaur with a large frill around its neck. However, it did not really have a frill, was not venomous and it would have been much larger than the dinosaur shown in the film.

Rhamphornhynchus

Rhamphornhynchus ('beak snout') was a long-tailed pterosaur that lived in the Jurassic period. The best preserved fossils of it were found in Bavaria, Germany, where many included traces of soft tissue such as wings. Rhamphornynchus fossils were also found in England, Tanzania and Spain.

It was most likely a cold-blooded animal. This is indicated by its growth rate, which was unlike warm-blooded animals like modern birds that can reach the size of an adult animal within their first year. Rhamphornhynchus needed a few years to become adult-sized.

Rhamphornhynchus was 1.2 meters (4.1 feet) long with a wingspan of 1.81 meters (5.9 feet) and it weighed just 2 kilograms. It had a long tail ending in a distinctive diamond-shaped vane. Its jaws contained needle-like teeth growing at an angle. However, the tip of its beak lacked teeth, which indicated that it mainly ate fish.

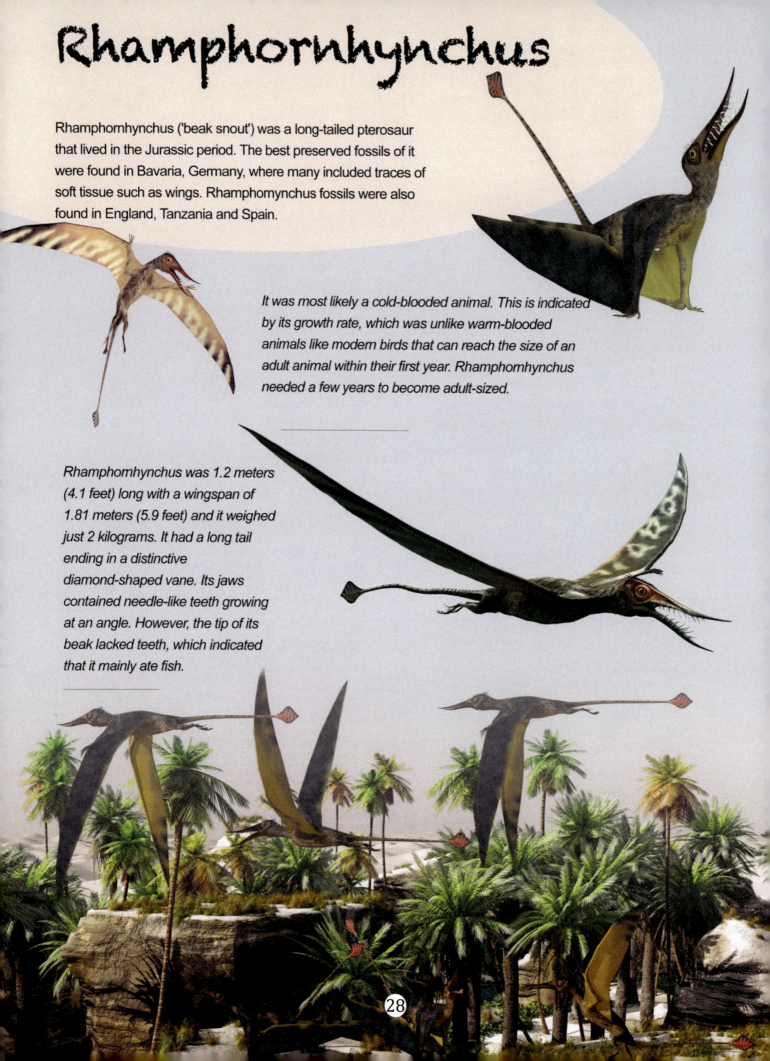

Allosaurus

Allosaurus ('different lizard') lived in the area of today's North America, Tanzania and Portugal approximately 155-145 million years ago. It was up 12 meters (39 feet) long and it weighed 4 tonnes. It would have been at the top of the food chain at the time and region where it lived.

There is much speculation regarding how Allosaurus hunted. It had a relatively weak jaw, with less force than today's lion or alligator, and also had small teeth. This indicates that it could not kill an adult sauropod with biting alone. Therefore, some scientists claim that it used its jaw like an axe: slashing prey with its teeth multiple times, causing them to eventually bleed to death. This is due to the high durability of the skull and large jaw width. Others claim that it ripped flaps of meat from living prey without killing them, repeating after they had recovered later. Its front limbs were probably used to hold its prey during the attack.

Allosaurus most likely hunted its prey in sudden bursts, like modern crocodiles with whom it shares a similar eye construction. Horn formations around the eyes would have limited its stereoscopic vision up to 20%.

Dimetrodon

Dimetrodon ('two measures of teeth') – was a carnivorous synapsid. It lived in today's southern area of the USA (mainly Texas, Oklahoma and New Mexico) around 280 million years ago. Dimetrodon's most recognisable feature was the large sail on its back formed by long neural spines extending from its vertebrae and covered with skin.

Dimetrodon was not actually a dinosaur although it is often mistaken for one. Dimetrodon belonged to the family of Sphenacodontidae. Research shows that Dimetrodon was more closely related to modern mammals than dinosaurs. It lived around 40 million before the first dinosaurs appeared.

Scientists have not yet established the exact function of the sail, however, it most likely helped regulate body temperature and intimidated predators.

Dimetrodon measured from 1.7 meters to 4.6 meters (5.6 to 15.1 feet) and weighed from 28 to 250 kilograms.

Dimetrodon was active during the day. It was a carnivore and ate other vertebrates smaller than itself. Although it was quick and agile it had widely spread limbs, similar to today's crocodiles, making it difficult to chase prey for an extended period. Like crocodiles, Dimetrodon most likely attacked its prey in sudden, surprising bursts.

Anhanguera

Anhanguera ('old devil') was a pterosaur that lived in the area of today's Brazil around 112 million years ago. Its wingspan was about 4.6 meters (15 feet).

It was most likely a fish-eating animal, catching its prey just below the surface of the water. However, it is possible that it also hunted insects in the air, and even fed on carcasses.

Anhanguera's skull was about 50 cm long with short, pointed teeth spread out along its beak. Like other pterosaurs, Anhanguera had a bone crest. Fossils found have had two distinct comb sizes. Either they belonged to two different species or the size change is characteristic of gender.

Giganotosaurus

Giganotosaurus was a theropod dinosaur, that lived around 98 to 97 million years ago (the Late Cretaceous period) in the area of today's Argentina. It is considered to be one of the largest, carnivorous land dinosaurs ever known. Some researchers have suggested that it was even larger than Tyrannosaurus, however, as no complete fossil of one has ever been found, it is hard to determine its exact size.

It is estimated that Giganotosaurus measured from 12 to 13 meters (39 to 43 feet) in length and weighed from 4.2 to 13.8 tonnes. Its skull is believed to be the biggest of all predatory dinosaurs, measuring from 1.53 to 1.80 meters (5.0 to 5.9 feet) in length, believed to be larger than a Spinosaurus' (1.5 to 1.75 meters long / 4.9 to 5.7 feet).

However, scientists are not entirely certain which dinosaur was larger - Giganotosaurus or T-Rex. Neither of them had an opportunity to meet and test the others' strength because the area where they lived and the era were completely different. Tyrannosaurus lived approximately 27-30 years million years after Giganotosaurus.

Deinonychus

Deinonychus ('Terrible Claw') was a carnivore. It lived 115-108 million years ago in the area of today's USA. It could reach up to 3.4 metres (11 feet) in length and 73 kilograms in weight. It was an agile and fast predator. Its long tail counterbalanced the weight of its body.

There used to be widespread opinion that Deinonychus was an extremely fast animal. However, more recent, accurate research suggests that it was in fact slower than the modern ostrich (top speed 70km/hour). The construction of its foot and the ratio of its size to the tibia bone suggest that what it sacrificed in speed it made up for in attacking skill, using the large talon on each lower limb.

Deinonychus belonged to a group of dinosaurs most closely related to modern birds to which it bears many similarities. It had bird-like anatomy and was most likely covered with feathers. It was through these discoveries that scientists began to see that birds evolved from dinosaurs.

Deinonychus probably lived and hunted its prey in herds. Although modern crocodiles and birds hunt alone, there is evidence that their predecessors may not have. Traces of Deinonychus teeth have been found in the bones of the much larger Tenontosaurus. A single Deinonychus would have been unable to kill a dinosaur of this size so it probably did not hunt alone.

Made in the USA
Coppell, TX
29 November 2019